GOT GEOGRAPHY!

POEMS SELECTED BY
Lee Bennett Hopkins

PICTURES BY
Philip Stanton

GREENWILLOW BOOKS
An Imprint of HarperCollins Publishers

To Hector, Paly, David, and Isabella Genao,
whether near or far . . .
—L. B. H.

To Massimiliana, Caterina, and Paola
—P. S.

Got Geography!
Text copyright © 2006 by Lee Bennett Hopkins
Illustrations copyright © 2006 by Philip Stanton

For information address HarperCollins Children's Books, a division of HarperCollins Publishers,
1350 Avenue of the Americas, New York, NY 10019.
www.harperchildrens.com

Graphite pencil on rag paper for the base drawing, watercolors and acrylic paints for the base painting,
and final touches using graphite crayons and watercolor crayons on top of the acrylic base were used
to prepare the full-color art. The text type is Stellar Classic.

Library of Congress Cataloging-in-Publication Data
Hopkins, Lee Bennett.
Got geography: poems / selected by Lee Bennett Hopkins; illustrated by Philip Stanton.
p.   cm.
"Greenwillow Books."
ISBN-10: 0-06-055601-3 (trade).   ISBN-13: 978-0-06-055601-3 (trade).
ISBN-10: 0-06-055602-1 (lib. bdg.)   ISBN-13: 978-0-06-055602-0 (lib. bdg.)
1. Geography—Juvenile poetry. 2. Children's poetry, American.
I. Hopkins, Lee Bennett. II. Stanton, Philip, ill.
PS595.G4G68 2006   811.008'032—dc22   2004059662

First Edition   10 9 8 7 6 5 4 3 2 1

Greenwillow Books

CONTENTS

Mapping the World

J. Patrick Lewis

I took my pens to *Africa*
Because a fire was in my brain,
And used their nibs acacia-fine
To paint the Serengeti Plain,
Victoria Falls, River Nile
Meandering past ancient folk.
This continent foreshadows all
The colors of a master's stroke.

When I had laid out *Europe* on
A canvas, it would teach me much
About such glories of a past
I painted Russian, Greek, and Dutch.
In pencil on my drawing board,
I traced *Australia's* seamless land—
Dreamtime of aborigines,
A walkabout through scrub and sand.

Let my skilled pen alone express
The thrill when *Asia* asked me in
To map astonishment, for here
Great Walls and history begin.
From fields of rice, my leap of faith
To field of ice, you hear me shout,
Antarctica!—pale continent.
My white ink practically ran out.

Which leaves me now to picture this:
I paint great nations lying South,
Canada and the fifty states.
Out of the wide, wide river's mouth—
Americas, Americas!—
Although the ink is not dry yet.
Geography is like our own
Room with a view we can't forget.

Latitude Longitude Dreams

Drew Lamm and James Hildreth

Magellan moved via stars
Steered his ship by celestial rays.
Columbus sailed on over the edge
Discovering lands and waterways.

They traversed their dreams, set their course
Voyaging over oceans and seas.
Etching earth with invisible designs
Crossing rivers, ice, and trees.

These lines that slide from pole to pole
Wrapping around the watery girth
Coordinate all of us on this globe
Our home, our ship, our planet earth.

.7

If I Were the Equator

Kathryn Madeline Allen

If I were the equator
I would have an attitude.
I'd boast the most about my no degrees of latitude.
I'd say, though there are other lines who run from east to west,
with nearly 25,000 miles I clearly am the best.
My equidistance from the poles,
I'd mention with a laugh,
makes me the one—the *only* one—who

splits the globe in half.
Smack dab
between the Tropics
with the sun high up above,
indeed,
I'd plead,
what on Earth could there be
about me *not* to love?

The Wonder of . . .

Rebecca Kai Dotlich

Geography:
An amazing, phenomenal way
to gather glorious Earth
from harbor, to basin, to bay,

from coastline, to canyon, to crater,
from tunnel, to tundra, to sea,
to dark, tangled patches of forest
resplendent with swampland and tree;

a billow of cascading waters,
a constantly breathtaking view
of cool falls tossing and tumbling
spilling their crystalline blue.

Behold! Massive mountain, deep mine,
wealthy with diamond and coal.
Meandering fjord, lone island.
One silent and chilly North Pole.

From continent to faraway continent,
by mile, by chartered degree;
this masterpiece of wonder:
Geography.

Awesome Forces

Joan Bransfield Graham

The earth is
        unsettled,
it would seem,
for here and about
it lets off
        steam,
lava flows,
geysers gush,
canyons are carved
        by a river's
        push.
The earth's old crust
cracks and creaks,
shakes and
        shoves up
        mountain
        peaks.
Ice caps recede,
glaciers advance,
ever in motion—
        a global dance.
        Will it ever
stand still?

        no chance

from North Atlantic

Carl Sandburg

The sea is always the same:
and yet the sea always changes.

    The sea gives all,
    and yet the sea keeps something back.

The sea takes without asking.
The sea is a worker, a thief, and a loafer.
    Why does the sea let go so slow?
    Or never let go at all?

The sea always the same
day after day
the sea always the same
night after night
fog on fog and never a star,
wind on wind and running white sheets,
bird on bird always a sea-bird—
so the days get lost:
it is neither Saturday nor Monday,
it is any day or no day,
it is a year, ten years.

Island   Isla

Francisco X. Alarcón

every island	todo isla
dreams	sueña
of being	con ser
a continent	un continente

The Mountain

David Harrison

"Approach if you dare,"
you say, knowing full well
how much we yearn
to stand on your highest peak
and gaze down on the world,
to dare!

"Climb my bony shoulders,"
you say, winking through clouds
you wear like a hat
on your cold white head.

"I'll clasp you to my breast
and when I let you go—
if I let you go—
you can tell your friends back home
you dared!"

For Forest

Grace Nichols

Forest could keep secrets
Forest could keep secrets

Forest tune in every day
to watersound and birdsound
Forest letting her hair down
to the teeming creeping of her forest-ground

But Forest don't broadcast her business
no Forest cover her business down
from sky and fast-eye sun
and when night come
and darkness wrap her like a gown
Forest is a bad dream woman

Forest dreaming about mountain
and when earth was young
Forest dreaming of the caress of gold
Forest rooting with mysterious eldorado

and when howler monkey
wake her up with howl
Forest just stretch and stir
to a new day of sound

but coming back to secrets
Forest could keep secrets
Forest could keep secrets
　　　　And we must keep Forest

18.

My Brother and I and the World

Mary Atkinson

My brother and I
ankle deep
in the cool water
of a brook
that tickled our legs
and spilled our buckets
as it ran into the sea
    decided
      to divide
        the world
        in half.

He got
the sandy bank
wavy ferns, wild blueberry bushes
pine trees, forest
and mountains all the way up to the sky

And I got
sea grass and rose hips
climbing rocks and tidal pools
splashing waves
and all of the ocean

All of the ocean, I told him
All the way around the world

Around the world, he asked
To my mountains and forests
To my blueberry bushes and sandy bank
Around the world to our brook
that turns into the sea?

My brother and I
sitting in the brook
on a hot summer's day
catching twigs and minnows
in our buckets
and letting wet sand
slide through our fingers and toes
    We decided
    not to divide
    the world
    in half
    but keep it as it was.

Early Explorers

Marilyn Singer

No place on earth
        is ever undiscovered
Even in Antarctica
        where whole mountains are hidden
                under ice
penguins already laid shambling tracks
                in the snow
        before we traveled there
The hottest desert
                the deepest jungle
        where none of us have ever been
all have been crossed
                and crossed again
        by wings whirring or silent
                feet furred or scaled
                        hoofed or bare
By adventurers we will never know
        explorers who will never tell us
                what wonders they have seen

A Map and a Dream

Karen O'Donnell Taylor

Maps are more
than tiny lines
intersecting
lace designs . . .
More than names
and colored dots,
rivers, mountains,
tourist spots.
Maps are keys
to secret places
vast new worlds
and unknown faces.
I can trace each
graceful line . . .
Close my eyes
and in my mind
I can travel
anywhere . . .
A map, a dream
can take me there!

Learning the World

Kristine O'Connell George

I'm memorizing oceans,
tracing rivers,
learning mountain ranges.
I'm memorizing capitals,
tracing countries,
learning crops and industries.

I'm smoothing out this map,
rolling it into a tube,
peering through one end,
wishing it were a telescope,
wishing I could see past my street,
wishing I could see
the whole world
spread beneath my feet.

Compass
Maria Fleming

Compass, compass,
Point the way
To wild places
Where few stray.
Across deep seas
To distant lands,
Toward arctic ice
And desert sands,
To jungles gleaming
Jewel-green,
To mountaintop
And deep ravine.
Guide me around
The globe and then,

Compass
Point me home again.

28.

Horizon

Jane Yolen

Just as the thin line
in a long division problem
divides the greater number
by the smaller,
horizon
divides earth and sky.

Gozinta, my mother called division,
explaining to me
the mysteries of math.
But earth does not gozinta sky,
held in place by horizon,
else we would all be flung,
unwilling, into the greater stars.

from
Lines Written for Gene Kelly to Dance To

Carl Sandburg

Why we got geography?

Because we go from place to place. Because the earth used
   to be flat and had four corners, and you could jump off
   from any of the corners.

But now the earth is not flat any more. Now it is round all
   over. Now it is a globe, a ball, round all over, and we
   would all fall off it and tumble away into space if it wasn't
   for the magnetic poles. And when you dance it is the
   North Pole or the South Pole pulling on your feet like
   magnets to keep your feet on the earth.

And that's why we got geography.

And it's nice to have it that way.

ACKNOWLEDGMENTS

For works in this collection, thanks are due to:

Kathryn Madeline Allen for "If I Were the Equator." Used by permission of the author, who controls all rights.

Mary Atkinson for "My Brother and I and the World." Used by permission of the author, who controls all rights.

Boyds Mills Press, Inc. for "The Mountain" from *Wild Country: Outdoor Poems for Young People*. Copyright © 1999 by David L. Harrison; "Horizon" from *Horizons: Poems As Far As the Eye Can See* by Jane Yolen. Copyright © 2002 by Jane Yolen. Both reprinted by permission of Wordsong, Boyds Mills Press, Inc.

Children's Book Press for "Island/Isla" from *From the Bellybutton of the Moon and Other Summer Poems* by Francisco X. Alarcón. Poem copyright © 1998 by Francisco X. Alarcón. Reprinted with permission of the publisher, Children's Book Press, San Francisco, CA. www.childrensbookpress.org

Curtis Brown, Ltd., for "The Wonder Of..." by Rebecca Kai Dotlich. Copyright © 2006 by Rebecca Kai Dotlich. Reprinted by permission of Curtis Brown, Ltd.

Curtis Brown Ltd., London, for "For Forest." Copyright © Grace Nichols, 1988. Reproduced with permission of Curtis Brown Ltd., London, on behalf of Grace Nichols.

Maria Fleming for "Compass." Used by permission of the author, who controls all rights.

Kristine O'Connell George for "Learning the World." Used by permission of the author, who controls all rights.

Joan Bransfield Graham for "Awesome Forces." Used by permission of the author, who controls all rights.

Harcourt, Inc., for an excerpt from "Lines Written for Gene Kelly to Dance To" in *Wind Song*, copyright © 1960 by Carl Sandburg and renewed 1988 by Margaret Sandburg, Janet Sandburg, and Helga Sandburg Crile; excerpt from "North Atlantic" in *Smoke and Steel* by Carl Sandburg, copyright © 1920 by Harcourt, Inc., and renewed 1948 by Carl Sandburg. Both reprinted by permission of the publisher.

Drew Lamm and James Hildreth for "Latitude Longitude Dreams." Used by permission of the authors, who control all rights.

J. Patrick Lewis for "Mapping the World." Used by permission of the author, who controls all rights.

Random House, Inc., for "Early Explorers" from *Footprints on the Roof: Poems About the Earth* by Marilyn Singer. Copyright © 2002 by Marilyn Singer. Used by permission of Alfred A. Knopf, an imprint of Random House Children's Books, a division of Random House, Inc.

Karen O'Donnell Taylor for "A Map and a Dream." Used by permission of the author, who controls all rights.